Our Teacher's Gone Bananas

Roisin

Best wishes

Jim Pike

Other books by John Foster

Our Teacher's Gone Bananas

Original poems by John Foster

Illustrated by Lizzie Finlay

OXFORD
UNIVERSITY PRESS

OXFORD

UNIVERSITY PRESS

Great Clarendon Street, Oxford OX2 6DP

Oxford University Press is a department of the University of Oxford.
It furthers the University's objective of excellence in research, scholarship,
and education by publishing worldwide in

Oxford New York

Auckland Bangkok Buenos Aires Cape Town
Chennai Dar es Salaam Delhi Hong Kong Istanbul Karachi
Kolkata Kuala Lumpur Madrid Melbourne Mexico City Mumbai
Nairobi São Paulo Shanghai Taipei Tokyo Toronto

Oxford is a registered trade mark of Oxford University Press
in the UK and in certain other countries

Database right Oxford University Press (maker)

First published 2004

British Library Cataloguing in Publication Data
Data available

ISBN 0 19 276317 2

1 3 5 7 9 10 8 6 4 2

Printed in Britain by
Cox & Wyman Ltd, Reading, Berkshire

Contents

Nests

Cockatoos make nests in shoes,
But parrots nest in carrots.
Budgerigars make nests in jars,
But parrots nest in carrots.

Puffins make their nests in muffins,
But parrots nest in carrots.
Arctic terns make nests in urns,
But parrots nest in carrots.

Nightingales make nests in veils,
But parrots nest in carrots.
Rooks make nests in library books,
But parrots nest in carrots.

Auntie Arabella

Auntie Arabella grows
Geraniums between her toes.

Twining round her legs and knees
Are various colours of sweet peas.

Sitting stately on her tum
Is a gold chrysanthemum.

Sprouting from her bulbous nose
Is a beautiful red rose.

Lovingly my uncle Ted
Tends her in her flower bed.

Loopy Lou and Potty Pete

Loopy Lou and Potty Pete
Wore shoes on their heads
And hats on their feet.
When they travelled into town
They always walked upside down.

On the Clip Clop Clap

(after Milligan)

On the Clip Clop Clap
All the Flops flip flap
And the Bongles boogle in the breeze.
The Sniggers snip snap,
The Trotters trip trap,
And the Somersaults sniff and sneeze
   The Somersaults sniff and sneeze.

On the Clip Clop Clap
You can never take a nap
For there's gnashing and there's thrashing in the trees,
As the Bongles flex their knees,
The Flops flip flap,
The Sniggers snip snap,
The Trotters trip trap,
And the Somersaults sniff and sneeze
   The Somersaults sniff and sneeze.

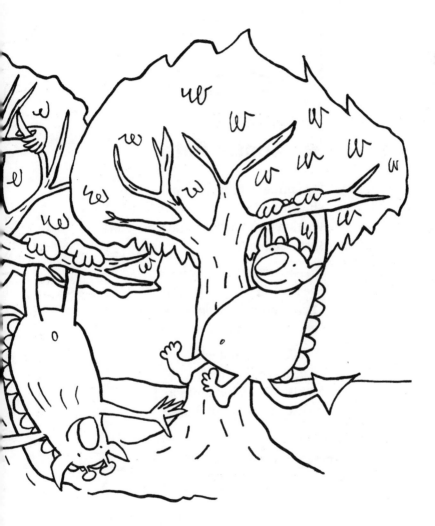

My Auntie Dot

My auntie Dot's a coffee pot.
She sits on the kitchen shelf,
Waiting for someone to take her down,
Muttering to herself.

'To be a coffee pot's my lot,'
She says. 'It's rather boring.
There's nothing to do, while I sit here,
I can't even practise pouring.

'A coffee pot is not what
I'd be if I could choose.
My sister's son has far more fun,
'Cause he's a pair of shoes!'

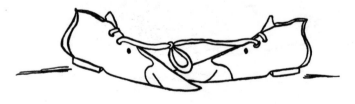

The Telephone's Got Toothache

The telephone's got toothache.
It keeps ringing with the pain,
Even when we switch it off.
There it goes again!

Please take it to the dentist.
It's driving me insane.
The telephone's got toothache.
It keeps ringing with the pain.

Par for the Course

When Auntie Fay began to neigh
And spend the day just eating hay,
My uncle said, 'It's par for the course.
Your auntie has become a horse.
I'll have to put her in the stable,
In the stall next to your auntie Mabel!'

Computer Cat

Computer Cat
Spends all day
Crouched at the ready,
Body tensed,
Eyes glued to the screen,
Tapping the keyboard
Till his paws ache,
Zapping mice.

Computer Cat
Spends all night
Stretched on the carpet,
Eyes shut, paws twitching,
Lost in a dream
Of chasing mice—
Too exhausted
To do the real thing.

The Curlapop

(after Milligan)

'What is a Curlapop, Dad?'
'It's a kind of a snake
Which lives in a box
And wears frilly socks
When it goes for a swim in the lake.'

'What does a Curlapop do, Dad?'
'It plays football with fleas.
It eats jellied eels
While turning cartwheels
And sings songs as it swings through the trees.'

'Have you seen a Curlapop, Dad?'
'On a day-trip to France,
In the town of Calais,
In a street café,
I once saw a Curlapop dance.'

'Are you sure there's a Curlapop, Dad?'
'Without any doubt, my son.
I swear by the moon
That goes green in June.
I'll take bets at a thousand to one.'

Zebedee Zero

In memory of Zebedee Zero
Who dreamed of being a sporting hero.
Alas he failed at every sport.
His efforts always came to nought.

The Truth About Wills

When you're living, your will can be secret.
No one needs to know what it will say.
But once you are gone, then everyone knows
For a will is a dead giveaway!

Uncle Frank

When we're all asleep in bed,
My uncle Frank unscrews his head.
He fixes on another one
And sets off for a night of fun.

It really gave me quite a jolt,
The first time that I saw the bolt,
Which Uncle proudly showed to me
In the cellar after tea.

He says the reason for his fame
Is that we share a famous name:
Oh, I forgot to tell you mine,
Our family's name is Frankenstein.

The Vampire's Apology

'I didn't mean to cause offence,'
Said the vampire with a grin.
'But when I saw you'd cut your face,
I just had to lick your chin!'

In Memory of Miss Chit-Chat

Beneath this stone Miss Chit-Chat lies,
Her gossiping days are done.
Her last words were as she passed away:
'I'm dying to tell someone.'

Epitaph

Here lies the body of a master baker:
Used to knead the dough,
Now needs an undertaker.

Elvis

My grandad thinks he's Elvis.
He's got this fake guitar.
He won it in a competition
In a karaoke bar.

He puts a black wig on,
And a shiny silver suit.
He thinks he is 'The King'.
We think he looks a hoot!

The Most Popular Style

When I go on the bus with Grandad,
Other children point and stare,
For on top of my grandad's head
There's hardly a single hair.

Sometimes they're rude and shout, 'Baldy',
But Grandad says with a smile,
'It's all the rage, when you're my age—
It's the most popular style!'

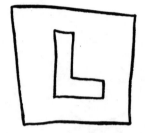

The Learner Bus

'Why has that bus got an L on it?' asked my little brother.
'Because it's a learner bus,' said Dad.
'I'm glad I'm not on it,' said my brother.
'I like buses to know where they're going.'

Ask No Questions

Ask no questions
Hear no lies
Our teacher's forgotten
To do up his flies!

Don't you look.
Don't you stare.
Teacher's wearing
Red underwear.

Our Teacher's Gone Bananas

Our teacher, Mr Mann,
Thinks he's an orang-utan.

When we do PE,
He climbs up the wall bars
And swings on the ropes.

When we do geography,
He talks about jungles
And gets a faraway look in his eyes.

When he takes assembly,
He hires a costume from Parties'R'Us
And talks about animal rights.

Our teacher has gone bananas.
There's nothing we can do.
Our teacher shouldn't be in a school,
He should be in a zoo!

Ask a Silly Question . . .

'Have you ever been inspected before?' I asked my teacher.
She scratched her head.
'No,' she said.
'I've never been inspected before, except for nits.'

A Pet to Be Proud Of

Our teacher's very proud of his pet.
There's a picture of it
Pinned on the board behind his desk.
It looks wonderful
Considering it's over eighty years old.
He keeps it locked up during the week,
But he always takes it out at weekends.
They've been to shows all over the country.
He's always washing and grooming it,
To make sure it's in tip-top condition.
Once a year he takes it
On a special day out
From London to Brighton.
There was a photograph of him
In the local paper
Standing beside it, smiling broadly.

Our teacher's very proud of his pet.
He says his pet's a star.
Our teacher's pet's a 1920s vintage Bentley car.

Locked Out

For Mrs H.

Our teacher's trapped in the playground.
She was late coming in from play.
The security door's been locked now.
She'll have to stay out all day!

Our teacher's trapped in the playground.
That's why she's got a big grin.
She's turning cartwheels and skipping about
'Cause she doesn't want to come in!

I Am a Question Mark

I am a question mark.
I sit on the keyboard
Waiting to be of service
In investigations and interrogations.
I help people with their enquiries.
If you're lost,
I can help you find the way.
If you're puzzled,
I can help you search for a solution.
If there's anything you need to know,
Just ask
And I'll show
That an answer's expected.

We Are the Tests

We are the tests that you must pass.
We decide who's top of the class.

We are the tests which tell how well
You're able to read and write and spell.

We are the tests. We find out too
Which maths questions you can do.

We are the tests. We're able to show
Which scientific facts you know.

We are the tests. You needn't be scared
So long as you are well prepared.

We are the tests examining you.
We will discover if it's true

That you have worked, not played the fool.
We are the tests. We rule the school.

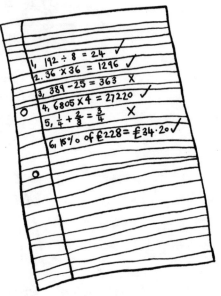

My Name is Term

My name is Term.
I fix the dates.
I decide when the school is to be open
And when it is to be closed.
Three times a year
I bring an end to holidays
And summon teachers and pupils
Back to their desks.
Within my boundaries
The school is a hive of activity.
When I am over
The corridors are empty
And the classrooms silent.
I am Term.
I bring the school to life.

The World's Best

My dad's the world's best.
He's a football referee.
He referees internationals
From a seat on our settee.

An hour before the kick off
He gets changed into his kit.
He then inspects the room
And tells us where to sit.

As we watch the pre-match build-up,
He waits beside the door,
Until the teams come out,
Then he strides across the floor.

He stands to attention
While the national anthems play,
Then takes his seat on the settee
As the game gets under way.

His eagle eyes spot every foul
The opposition makes.
He's very quick to point out
The real ref's mistakes.

He won't stand for any nonsense.
On dissent he's very hard.
If we challenge his decisions,
He shows us a red card.

But sometimes he forgets
His self-appointed role
By letting out a mighty roar
When England score a goal.

My Mum Says

My mum says:

If you don't pick up your pyjamas
and fold them under your pillow,
I'll throw them out of the window
for the dustmen to pick up.

If you don't go upstairs
and get washed immediately,
I'll take you out into the garden
and turn the hosepipe on you.

If you don't hurry up and get dressed,
I'll take you to school
in your knickers.

If you're not out of this door
in ten seconds' time,
I'll kiss you goodbye outside school.

My mum says:

You think I'm joking, don't you!

Grandad Says

Grandad says
His team are the strongest team
In the entire football league.
'How's that?' I ask,
Looking at the table
And pointing out their position—
Bottom of the third division.
'Exactly!' he says.
'They are supporting
All the teams above them!'

Grandma says
Grandad is their strongest supporter.
'Why's that?' I ask.
Grandma laughs,
'Because he's their only supporter!'

Nonsense Football Rhymes

United's Red

United's red.
City's blue.
The ref needs glasses
And so do you.

Little Jack Horner

Little Jack Horner took a shot.
The goalie was unsighted.
Jack Horner scored.
The crowd all roared.
They'd beaten Man United!

Old King Cole

Old King Cole was a very fine manager,
A very fine manager was he.
He didn't believe in 4–4–2.
He always played 4–3–3.

Each of his teams had very fine strikers,
Oh, very fine strikers had he.
No team was there
That could compare
With King Cole and his strikers three.

Wee Willie Winkie

Wee Willie Winkie jumps up and down
In front of the TV in his nightgown,
Yelling with delight as the captain steps up
To score from the spot and win the World Cup.

Mary Had a Cockerel

Mary had a cockerel,
Which came from White Hart Lane
And every time that Tottenham scored
It crowed and crowed again.

Save-a-shot, Save-a-shot, Goalie Man

Save-a-shot, save-a-shot, goalie man.
Kick it upfield as far as you can.
Dive on it. Pounce on it. Block it with your feet.
Push it round the post and keep a clean sheet.

Saturdays

Every Saturday, it's the same—
Worrying about the game.
Will we win? Will we draw?
Will we lose? Who will score?

Some Saturdays I get the blues,
That's because United lose.
Some Saturdays I get to grin,
That's because United win.

Kicking In

I'm kicking my ball
against the wall
against the wall and back.

I'm practising how
to pass the ball
by kicking the ball
against the wall
against the wall and back.

I'm practising how
to launch an attack
by passing the ball
against the wall
and running to get it back.

I'm dribbling the ball
towards the wall
around the dustbin and back.

I'm beating defenders
one and all
as I dribble the ball
towards the wall
around the dustbin and back.

I imagine the goalie
coming out.
I hear the fans
all cheer and shout.
I shoot the ball
towards the wall.
He dives too late.
It's through the gate!
And I've scored! I've scored! I've scored!

Please, Mr Black

Mr Black, Mr Black,
Please can we have our football back?
You can pass it through the window.
It'll fit through the crack.
Oh, don't be a spoilsport, Mr Black.
Please give us our football back.

More Nonsense Football Rhymes

Pop Goes the Arsenal!

Up and down to Highbury,
In and out the turnstiles,
That's the way the fans all go,
Pop goes the Arsenal!

Half a pound of Henry's tricks,
Half a pound of Kanu's,
That's the way the goals are scored,
Pop goes the Arsenal!

Doctor Selsey went to Chelsea

Doctor Selsey went to Chelsea
In a shower of rain.
He felt so ill when they lost five–nil
That he never went there again.

Hey, Diddle Diddle

Hey, diddle diddle, the cat and the fiddle,
The manager's over the moon.
We've just qualified for the Champions League,
He'll be offered a new contract soon.

Little Jumping Billy

Here am I, little jumping Billy.
When I scored an own goal,
I felt very silly.

Bobby Shaftoe

Bobby Shaftoe went over the sea
Went to play in Italy
Got a massive transfer fee—
Lucky Bobby Shaftoe.

The Man in the Wilderness

The man in the Wilderness asked of me:
Who will the League Champions be?
I answered him as I was able:
The team that finishes top of the table.

When Grandma Sat on a Staple

When Grandma sat on a staple,
She shot in the air with a shriek.
Where her knickers were thin,
It pierced the skin
And left a blue bruise on her cheek.

Uncle Don

Uncle Don, Uncle Don,
Why haven't you got your trousers on?
Oh dear, I forgot 'em
That's why you can see my bottom!

At the School for Pantomime Horses

At the school for pantomime horses,
It's not surprising to find
That everyone wants to be the front
And no one to be the behind.

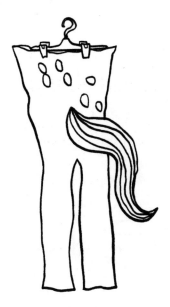

A Fatal Mistake at Giant School

During a lesson on safety
A young giant sitting at the back
Fell asleep and missed hearing the warning:
Beware of a young boy called Jack.

Interview with a Dragon

What's your name?
Firesnorter.
I'm Thunderflash and Firecracker's daughter.

Where were you born?
In Stalactite Cavern,
High on the hill above Flamethrowers Tavern.

What games do you like playing?
Maiden-chasing, Fight-a-Knight,
and Try to Set the Torch Alight.

Which football team do you support?
Cave City Rovers—the best team by far
With Toaster, their ten-million goalscoring star.

What are your favourite foods?
Mammoth and chips and roasted boggart
And ten-litre buckets of gorse-flavoured yoghurt.

What are your favourite drinks?
Hot gearbox oil. Runny boiling custard
And 5-Star petrol spiced with mustard.

What are your favourite videos?
'The Last Crusader'.
'Knights on Fire' and 'The Scorched Invader'.

What are your hobbies?
Collecting treasure. Painting caves.
Stealing princesses as slaves.

What is your ambition?
To set the world on fire.
To conquer knights.
To see my name up there in lights.

A Big Mistake

My owner's made a big mistake.
He thinks I'm not a poisonous snake.
I'm waiting till the time is right
To give him just a tiny bite,
To let him know a snake like me
Should not be in captivity.

Animal Apologies

'Sorry,' said the kangaroo.
'I shouldn't have jumped to conclusions.'

'Sorry,' said the camel.
'I can't help it. I've always got the hump.'

'Sorry,' said the dog.
'I've been barking up the wrong tree.'

'Sorry,' said the electric eel.
'I got my wires crossed.'

'Sorry,' said the donkey.
'I'm always making an ass of myself.'

'Sorry,' said the giraffe.
'I shouldn't have stuck my neck out.'

'Sorry,' said the crocodile.
'I shouldn't have snapped.'

No Hard Feelings

'I'm sorry,' said the apple
As it bounced off Newton's head.
'I didn't see you standing there.
You really should have said.'

'Don't apologize,' said Newton.
'Although my head is sore,
You have shown me that gravity
Is just a natural law.'

Introductions 1: Del

Hello, I'm called Del and these are my friends.
They're all called Del, too!

This one's always pleased to meet you.
He'll bring a smile to your face:
Del-ight.

But take care with the second one.
He's frail and fragile:
Del-icate.

The third one's a bit of a lad.
Always getting into scrapes:
Del-inquent.

The next one's a bit excitable.
He's apt to see things that aren't there:
Del-irious.

As for me, haven't you guessed?
I'm the pick of the bunch.
Sweet-smelling and mouthwatering:
Del-icious.

Introductions 2: Phil

Hello, I'm called Phil and these are my friends.
They're all called Phil, too!

This one's very fond of music.
He plays in the orchestra and sings in the choir.
He's Phil-harmonic.

This one's obsessed with his hobby.
He's into stamp collecting.
He's Phil-ately.

This one works for a charity.
He's kind and benevolent.
He's Phil-anthropic.

This is the scholarly one.
He works in a university analysing texts.
He's Phil-ologist.

Finally, there's me, wise and thoughtful.
I keep calm, taking things as they come:
I'm Phil-osophical.

Introductions 3: Al

Hello, I'm called Al and these are my friends.
They're all called Al, too.

This one's a famous wizard.
He's always concocting new potions in search
of the elixir of life.
He's Al-chemist.

This one's a musician, a singer.
He also plays the saxophone and the flute.
He's Al-to.

This one's a mathematician.
He solves equations by using symbols to
represent numbers.
He's Al-gebra.

$$1, \quad 3x + 2 = 8$$
$$3x = 8 - 2$$
$$x = \frac{8 - 2}{3}$$
$$x = 2$$

This one's a real friend. Someone you can trust.
He'll stand up for you whatever happens.
He's Al-ly.

You can count on me, too.
I'm genuinely concerned about the welfare of others.
I'm Al-truist.

$$2, \quad 3x = y = 10$$
$$2x = 2y = 12$$
$$3x = 10 = y$$
$$x = \frac{10 - y}{3}$$
$$2x + 2y = 12$$
$$x + y = \frac{12}{2}$$
$$x + y = 6$$
$$x = 2$$
$$y = 4$$

A Question of Names

Why is Pip like Pop
But Bob not like Rob?
Why is Mum like Dad
But Nan not like Gran?

Why is Anna like Hannah
But Eve not like Steve?
Why is Ada like Otto
But Lil not like Jill?

Two Tongue Twisters

Underwood's Underwear
Underwood would wear underwear
If Underwood knew where
Underwood put
Underwood's underwear.

Did Underwood put his underwear
Under here or over there?
Did Underwood put his underwear
Under or over the chair?

I wonder, wonder where,
Underwood put
Underwood's underwear?

Sue Shore Shrieked
Sue Shore shrieked.
Sue Shore shouted, 'Shoo!'
Sue was sure she saw
A shrew in her shoe.

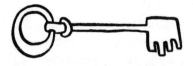

A Fortunate Find

The first of you comes last of all
And the last of all is first.
The last of you is second, too
And the third of second is third.
The first of key is second to last
And so is the last of unlock.

Solve this puzzle and you'll see
How fortunate a word can be.

Dotty Definitions

Illegal: a bird of prey that is not very well.

Crowbar: a place where crows meet for a drink.

Bedlam: a cuddly sheep which sings a lullaby.

Category: a cat that has been in a fight.

Ramshackle: a sheep that has been tied up.

Bulldozer: a bull which is taking a nap.

Hobbyhorse: a horse that won't stop talking about stamp collecting.

Dormant: an ant which sleeps in a dormitory.

Dogma: what a dog's mother believes.

Toadstool: an implement used by a toad; also a piece of furniture in a toad's house.

Spelling Mnemonic

Most	Many	Make up
Nude	Naughty	Nonsensical acrostics:
Elephants	Eels	Easily
Munch	Make	Memorize
Only	Odious	Odd
Nice	Noises	New spellings
Iced	In	In
Carrots	Cafés	Comfort

whatspunctuation

whatspunctuationweallneed
itsothatwecanread
whatotherswritewithoutitwed
besoconfusedwewouldnotknow
ifweshouldstoporgo
onreadingwewouldlosetheflow
ofwhatthewritermeanttosay
yeswedallloseourway
sopunctuationsheretostay

Dads Views' on Apostrophe's

Apostrophe's often appear in place's
where they are not mean't to,
like in grocery shop's windows'
advertising orange's and apple's,
or they are omitted when they shouldnt be.
Its all very confusing, isnt it?
Dad say's if hed got any say
(which he hasnt)
hed abolish the bloomin thing's.

Commas

Commas like, apostrophes
often, appear in places
where, they shouldn't,
But Dad, says
they are a different,
kettle of fish,
you need, to know
how to use, them properly,
you shouldn't just scatter them,
everywhere like, confetti,

Staircase Poem

This is a staircase poem.
Can you find your way down,
Making very, very
Sure that you see the letter,
Especially placed on each step,
Indicating that you must
Not hurry, but
Take special *care*.

A Collection of Collectives

A punnet of puns
A likeness of similes
A kayak of palindromes
An anteroom of prefixes
A chatter of speech marks
A surprise of exclamations
A halt of full stops
A column of silent letters.

Word Building

The Word Wizard said:
Once again start with nothing:
O.
Put an l in front
And behold what you have is:
Lo.
Fix on a w
And make yourself scarce by lying like this:
Low.
Now add an s.
You may as well take your time.
You'll find yourself going at a snail's pace:
Slow.
Mix in a b and shake.
But take care.
You want to avoid coming to this:
Blows.
Now you need an e.
But don't be pushy.
Keep them to your sides:
Elbows.
Finally, take another l
And you can use them to get a fire going,
Or else you can make noises like any angry bull:
Bellows.

Riddle

My first is in ghoul and also in charm.
My second is in magic and twice in alarm.
My third is in cauldron but isn't in fire.
My fourth is in gremlin but not in vampire.
My fifth is in skeleton and in bones.
My sixth is in werewolf but isn't in groans.
My seventh is in spell but not in broomstick.
My eighth's found in treat, but not found in trick.
My ninth is in phantom but isn't in fear.
My whole is the scariest night of the year.

Sir K

I am a silent k.
Without me
Someone might nick your knickers
Or nap in your knapsack.
You need me to be able to knead,
To knock or to kneel.
I can help you
To knuckle down to knitting.
I have the knack.
Sir K, that's me—
A knowledgeable knight!

Going Quietly

When a ptarmigan goes to the loo,
He makes less noise than you or I do.
The reason's plain, you see,
He has a silent p.

The Silent Gees

The silent gees are coming.
They may be gnearing you.
The gnarled gnome, the gnashing gnat
And the gnasty, gnawing gnu.

The silent gees are coming.
There's gnot much you can do,
Except to feed them gnocchi
And gnotify the zoo.

The Dragon-Diner

I'm a twenty-first century dragon,
I run the Dragon-Diner.
If it's fast-food that you want,
You won't find any finer.

With a flick of the flame
From my fiery lips
I can sizzle you up
A steak and chips.

Beefburgers, bacon,
Crisp, crunchy fish,
Potato cakes, ham and eggs,
Name your dish!

I'm faster than a microwave.
There's no food finer.
If it's fast-food that you want,
Come to the Dragon-Diner.

The Man With a Map

Sitting in a bar
In many a seaside town
You'll see a man with a faraway look,
His face creased into a frown.

He looks a scruffy sort.
His shirt is tattered and torn.
His hair is greasy and matted.
His boots are scuffed and worn.

Tattooed on his forearm,
There's a skull and crossbones flag
And on the floor, beside his chair,
There's an ancient canvas bag.

In front of him on the table,
A parchment map is spread.
As he scrutinizes it closely,
He slowly shakes his head.

He's searching for the spot
Where they dug a hole and hid
The chests that held the treasure
Plundered by Captain Kidd.

But the ink on the map has faded.
The paper is cracked and dry.
As he looks in vain for a cross,
He heaves a heavy sigh.

You can see him in a bar
In many a seaside town,
A pirate with a faraway look,
His face creased into a frown.

Barnacle Bill

Barnacle Bill's a millionaire.
He owns a chain of stores
Selling exotic merchandise
Plundered from faraway shores.

Visit Barnacle's website
At BarnacleB.com,
Find lots of fabulous bargains
For people to choose from.

If it's something gruesome you're after
Try Barnacle's 'Treasure Trove':
Buy a bloodstained bandanna
Or bones from Deadman's Cove.

If it's something for your ladyfriend,
Barnacle B's is the place.
There're jewels galore, rings by the score,
Silks and satins and lace.

But be sure to take plenty of cash.
Bill doesn't believe in a bank.
The last person to ask for credit
Was made to walk the plank.

Barnacle Bill's a millionaire.
He owns a chain of stores
Selling exotic merchandise
Plundered from faraway shores.

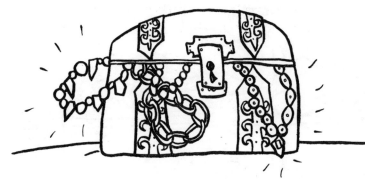

The Poolside Pirates

The pirates sit beside their pools
In Beverley Hills, LA,
Swigging rum, playing 'Walk the Plank',
And passing the time of day.

For the pirates all are film stars now.
They're stars of the silver screen.
They get the parts they're made for—
The parts where you've got to look mean.

The pirates are cast as gangsters,
As vampires, werewolves, and crooks.
The nastier and uglier the characters are—
Then the pirates have got the looks.

So you needn't pity the pirates.
The pirates are doing OK,
As they sit and polish their Oscars at home
In Beverley Hills, LA.

Love Letter–From the Wizard to the Witch

I find your looks bewitching,
The way you stand and glare.
I love the way you shake your locks
Of tangled, matted hair.

I find your smile enchanting,
Your wicked, evil grin.
It makes me want to touch and stroke
Your gnarled and wrinkled skin.

I find your face spellbinding,
The warts upon your cheek,
So hairy, black, and crusty—
They make my knees go weak.

I find you so enthralling.
I love your witchy smell
Of rats and dung and sewers—
You hold me in your spell!

We've a Pet Pterodactyl

We've a pet pterodactyl.
We keep it in the attic.
When it flaps its wings
It makes an awful racket.

We've a pet pterodactyl.
We've locked it in a cage.
It squawks and it screeches.
It's always in a rage.

Don't get a pterodactyl
And keep it as a pet.
It bites you when you feed it.
It even bit the vet!

We've a pet pterodactyl.
We'd really like to sell it.
But no one wants to buy it.
Who can blame them once they smell it!

The Slinky Snurgle

Beware the Slinky Snurgle
It's sneaky and it's sly.
It creeps upon and leaps upon
Unwary passers-by.

It stretches out its tentacles
And gives a wicked grin.
It slavers as it searches for
A place to pierce your skin.

Beware the Slinky Snurgle
With its cracked and warty lips.
It wraps you in its tentacles
Then sucks and slurps and sips.

The Snow Monster

When the snow monster sneezes,
Flurries of snow swirl and whirl,
Twisting round trees, curling into crevices,
Brushing the ground a brilliant white.

When the Snow Monster bellows,
Blizzards blot out the sky,
Piling up drifts, blocking roads,
Burying the landscape in a white grave.

When the Snow Monster cries,
Soft flakes slip and slide gently down
Into the hands of waiting children
Who test their taste with their tongues.

When the Snow Monster sleeps,
The air crackles with children's laughter
As they throw snowballs, build snowmen,
And whizz downhill on their sledges.

The Frightening Phantom

Deep in the Forest of Fear
The Frightening Phantom waits
To pounce on Careless Children
Who stray Beyond the Gates.

Through the Forest of Fear
The Frightening Phantom glides.
In the Dark and Gloomy Glen
The Frightening Phantom hides.

In the Heart of the Forest of Fear
The Frightening Phantom lurks.
The Frightening Phantom snatches.
The Frightening Phantom smirks.

Beware the Frightening Phantom
Which lives in the Forest of Fear.
Take heed of the Witch's Warning:
DON'T GO NEAR!

The Prisoner

In a dank dark dungeon
in the Castle of Despair,
the Prisoner kneels
muttering a prayer.

In a cold clammy cell
the Prisoner lies,
the Prisoner shivers,
the Prisoner sighs.

Through fevered nights
the Prisoner dreams
of woodland glades
and cooling streams.
The Prisoner screams.

In a dank dark dungeon
in the Castle of Despair,
the Prisoner kneels
muttering a prayer.

We Are the Gremlins

We are the gremlins.
We're up to no good.
We do things we shouldn't,
Not things that we should.

We get up to mischief
Of every sort.
But we're cunning and clever
And never get caught.

We are the gremlins.
We disconnect wires.
We slip chains off bikes
And let down your tyres.

We guide balls through windows.
We hide little things,
Like pieces of jigsaws.
We tie knots in strings.

We separate socks.
We tear your new skirt,
Unpeg clothes from the line
And roll them in dirt.

We hide deep inside
Every kind of machine.
We scramble the text
On your computer screen.

We change all the channels
On your video,
So you record the news
Not your favourite show.

We set your alarm clock
For half-past eight,
So you oversleep
And get to school late.

We are the gremlins.
We're up to no good.
We do things we shouldn't,
Not things that we should.

We get up to mischief
Of every sort.
But we're cunning and clever
And never get caught.

I Am Fighting This Poem

I am fighting this poem
Knitting at a cable,
Cruising a hen
And a niece of taper.
The birds are all in a huddle,
So I mope you can
Shirk out its leaning.

Index of Titles and First Lines

(First lines are in italic)